MATSURI

MATSURI

World of Japanese Festivals

Gorazd Vilhar
Charlotte Anderson

SHUFUNOTOMO CO., LTD.
Tokyo, Japan

Book design by Toshiaki Suzuki

First printing, 1994
Third printing, 2000

Published by Shufunotomo Co., Ltd.
2–9, Kanda Surugadai, Chiyoda-ku
Tokyo, 101-8911 Japan

Printed in Japan

ISBN 4–07–976066–3

祭 MATSURI

They are, perhaps, the ultimate celebrations. Amid a spectacular display of costume, color, and age-old ritual, participants summon the gods down to earth to mingle and rejoice with them. A most eloquent form of worship, Japanese festivals are intimate, joyous encounters with the divine.

Japan may well enjoy more festivals than any other country in the world. On almost any day of the year, at least one festival is sure to be under way somewhere on the archipelago, and on certain days, the whole nation seems to be in the thick of celebration. Varying in size and grandeur, some *matsuri* may involve no more than a single part-time priest and the handful of residents of a tiny farming village modestly celebrating spring planting; others may engage a cast of more than a thousand to thrill tens of thousands of onlookers with their pageantry. They encompass celebrations both rural and urban, traditional and modern, solemn and fun.

Originally, and still predominantly, Shinto observances, *matsuri* came also to include certain calendrical rites of Chinese Buddhist origin. But whether Shinto or Buddhist at heart, elements of both are often present at any one event.

Prevailing images of modern Japan tend to minimize the significance of these ancient religious practices. Yet they have long provided the people with a strong spiritual identity and continue to hold an honored place in Japanese life. Considerable insight into contemporary Japan can be gained from a knowledge and understanding of these spiritual roots which continue to sustain the nation through its technological, political, and social changes.

Although many Japanese people are inclined to declare to foreigners that they have no religion at all, that conviction seems to arise from a difference in terms. Japanese interpretation of the term "religion" generally presupposes a founder, a doctrine which excludes all others, a holy book, a weekly holy day—elements which certain other religions possess but theirs, largely, do not. Simply put, the Japanese consider Buddhism more a philosophy than a religion, and Shinto, a spiritually integrated way of life.

Shinto (the way of the gods) is an indigenous and animistic faith with its origins deep in the mists of time. Its central theme is the veneration of the life force, which is nature, and of Amaterasu Ōmikami, nature's creator and the progenitor of the Japanese imperial line. She is the Great Divinity Illuminating Heaven, goddess of the sun.

Shinto gods, the divine forces, are called *kami*. Existing in immense numbers, they are manifest in all things, animate and inanimate, and pervade all aspects of human life. It is believed that the world functions through the cooperation of the *kami* and their believers and strives toward the social harmony in which the gods rejoice. The *kami* are linked inextricably to the Japanese psyche, so much so that it has been said that without Japan there would be no Shinto, and without Shinto, no Japan. In the distant past, it helped the Japanese to define their role in the immediate world. Today it serves as a grounding force for a people who, in times of great change, are trying to hold on to their identity, as well as to redefine their relationship with a far broader and more complex world. Inseparable from daily life, Shinto is observed in a multitude of acts, ceremonies, and festivals throughout the year.

Although *kami* faith stretches far back into Japanese history, it was given the name Shinto in the eighth century, and then only to differentiate it from the growing popularity of Buddhism and other imported beliefs and philosophies. Buddhism, although born in India, arrived in Japan from China by way of Korea in the sixth century. Introduced as only one part of the vastly superior Chinese culture that so awed the Japanese, it was enthusiastically taken up by the imperial court as a faith with possible greater divine powers than those of their native gods. It took several centuries for Buddhism to reach the Japanese commoner but when it did, it flourished. In a form more Japanese than Chinese or Indian, Buddhism has been a substantial force in Japan for a millennium.

After an initial rivalry, Shinto and Buddhism settled into a largely peaceful coexistence, with Shinto gods often viewed as local manifestations of Buddhist deities, rather than competitors. Indeed, Buddhism has a history of accommodating itself to local faiths. The religions mingled and even at times merged, so that the line between the two can still often be a little blurred. However, the two belief systems are very different from one another, so each has its own niche to fill. The realm of Shinto is the cycle of nature, the seasons, and everyday life, while Buddhism's domain is death and afterlife.

Although a relatively small nation, Japan supports some 75,000 Buddhist temples and 100,000 Shinto shrines, both small and large, modest and grand. These remarkable numbers say much about the respect given to the spiritual side of life in Japan. The vast majority of people call upon each religion as needed and without any sense of personal conflict, for their gods are not jealous gods. In a mutually beneficial relationship, the gods serve the people, and the people serve the gods, giving them their due at the proper time, at the proper place, and in the proper way. These various acts of worship culminate in the celebration of *matsuri*. Derived from the verb *matsuru* (to worship), *matsuri* serve as a means for the people to offer the divine world their prayers, gifts, reverence, and joy.

The festival is many things to the Japanese people: an opportunity for communion with their gods and ancestral spirits; an avowal of their common past, which reaches far back into mythical times; a celebration of nature and the renewing cycle of the seasons; and, not least of all, an excuse for exuberant merrymaking with family and neighbors, thereby reaffirming communal bonds and providing welcome relief from the work and regimentation of daily life.

A great many of the *matsuri* are related to rice growing, the very foundation of Japanese culture. Others honor the guardian deities of clans, villages, towns, and districts. Still others range from celebrations of national history and culture to more individual and family-oriented festivals.

As primary as is the cultivation of rice to the Japanese people, so are the festivals which guard and celebrate that process. Rites connected to the agricultural cycle are held throughout most of the country and span all four seasons. The gods are petitioned for a favorable growing season, to drive away pests and natural disasters which could harm the burgeoning grain, while later in the year, thanks are given for a bountiful harvest. Extremely varied in form and accouterment, these festivals are bound by their common purpose.

In winter, farming communities all over Japan begin to enact primeval rites to invoke the favor of the deities upon their upcoming labors. Every February, in the northern prefecture of Aomori, for example, the farmers of Hachinohe gather to perform a dance of fertility, stomping the snow-covered earth to call it to life. Splendid headdresses worn by these Emburi Matsuri dancers bear the painted images of Inari, the god of grains, and Ebisu, a god of prosperity.

Spring brings numerous ceremonies to seek continued fortune for the cultivation process. Typical of events undertaken elsewhere, the rice planting around Nara is preceded by a spring festival at Kasuga Shrine, where *miko* (sacred shrine maidens) enact the planting process in stylized dance. Their virginity symbolizes the fertility which is sought for the young rice shoots. In this act of imitative magic, all stages of growth are represented and ritually brought to fulfillment, thereby petitioning the same auspicious denouement for the actual crops.

With the rains of early summer, followed by the intense, sometimes enervating, midsummer heat, community festivals continue to beseech the *kami* for heedfulness to their precious crops. Kawase Matsuri in Chichibu exemplifies that season's celebratory supplications which seek not only the continued growth and safety of their rice crops, but heavenly protection for the health of the people. The spirit of the deity, ordinarily enshrined at Chichibu Shrine, is ceremonially transferred to the *mikoshi* (portable shrine). After carrying it in parade to the river, its bearers immerse it and boisterously splash around in the water to give the god a ritual bath and, at the same time, to entertain him. He returns the favor soon, when golden autumn brings paddies heavy with grain. Meanwhile, the people revel with their god and take pleasure in this brief but welcome break in their workaday routine.

When the abundant harvest is in, it is again time to remember the gods. Autumn festivals abound, and some of the best of them are at the ubiquitous Inari shrines, where the deity of grains is worshiped. In Shinto, certain animals are regarded as messengers of the gods, and at Inari shrines, it is the white fox. In an interesting syncretic observance, the Buddhist temple Hōjōji in Yamaguchi Prefecture celebrates an annual autumn Kitsune-no-Yomeiri (Foxes' Wedding Procession). A costumed and masked fox-bride and fox-groom are ritually married in celebration of a long-ago miracle, when a pair of old foxes died and attained buddhahood. In honor of the foxes' long, faithful life together, young women take part in the procession, hoping that it will lead them to long and faithful marriages, too. But this is rice country, and the Shinto association with foxes is unmistakable, particularly with a small Inari shrine right on the temple grounds. With harvest prayers and an altar laid with offerings of new rice, the event's supplementary dedications are those of a Shinto harvest festival.

Other livelihoods are not forgotten. The deities are implored to provide fishermen with abundant catches by means of *matsuri* held in many coastal fishing towns and villages. In Ōhara on the Pacific coast of the Bōsō Peninsula, this plea takes the form of Hadaka Matsuri, the so-called Naked Festival, in which the area's fishermen, dressed only in *fundoshi* (loincloths), bear eighteen god-dwelling *mikoshi* into the ocean waves.

Festivals may focus on other elements of nature, too. The beauty of nationally revered blossoms, the advent of the autumnal full moon, or the continued rest of the sleeping volcano Mount Fuji, for example, are celebrated in *matsuri* around Japan.

Life's milestones may also be observed in festival form. Celebrated nationwide on November 15 is the beloved childhood festival Shichi-Go-San (Seven-Five-Three). On that day, or on a near weekend, boys of age five and girls of ages three and seven are taken to their local shrines to be blessed with the divine protection of their guardian deity or, as has recently become fashionable, to a grander shrine of particular importance to make the event even more memorable. The tots are dressed in their finest. For girls that often means a diminutive but spectacular kimono with all the required accessories—a major parental investment for the sake of beauty, tradition and, again, memories.

Major among the family-oriented festivals celebrated nationwide is the summer Festival of the Dead, O-Bon. An event of the ancient Chinese

Buddhist calendar, it has been celebrated in Japan since the seventh century. With lanterns or fires to light their way, the spirits of ancestors are welcomed home from the world beyond for a three-day visit. Family members return to their hometowns to reunite with one another and to honor their ancestors. In villages, towns, and urban neighborhoods, outdoor folk dances called *bon odori* are performed by residents who are often charmingly attired in the colorful cotton *yukata* and wooden *geta* of summer evenings of old. Originally intended as entertainment for the visiting spirits, today this ancient custom has become more an enjoyable social event for the living. It nevertheless still embodies the essence of O-Bon, a happy time for families in their continuing and satisfying relationship with the spirits of their ancestors and departed loved ones.

Reenactments of legends and historical moments dear to the people comprise yet another category of the countless festivals celebrated each year throughout Japan. One of the grandest, Kyoto's Gion Matsuri sprang from a plea by Emperor Seiwa to the *kami* enshrined at Yasaka Shrine to bring to an end the devastating plague of the summer of 869. When it duly abated, the city held a great festival of thanksgiving to the deity, featuring a hand-drawn wheeled pavilion topped with medieval halberds.

In the year 970, that festival was instituted as an annual event, in praise and continuing petition of the illustrious *kami* who had brought the land salvation a century before. Year by year, century by century, the event gained in splendor, with more numerous pavilions acquiring ever more features and embellishments. Today these floats are of the finest construction and bear a wealth of treasured antique art objects, mechanical historical figures, and elaborated scenes, as well as bands of musicians playing the hypnotic flute, drum and *shamisen* music called Gion-bayashi. Over thirty majestic floats are drawn by teams of straining, *happi*-coated men and accompanied in procession by many hundreds of gloriously costumed men, women, and children.

Riding high on the lead float is the *chigo* (the celestial child), a pre-pubescent boy carefully selected and ritually sanctified to be acceptable to the god. Indeed, it is the *chigo* who will embody the *kami* spirit during this festival. And it is his ritual act of perfectly severing the sacred rope (*shimenawa*) to formally open the procession which will ensure the god's blessings upon the city for the coming year.

For the sight-seeing multitudes who have come from across Japan to view this spectacle, the procession *is* the festival. But for citizens of Kyoto, natives of the city for generations upon generations, that is only one grand element in a month-long choreographed drama of history, religion and, not least of all community pride. Something more than a festival, Gion Matsuri with all its rites and trappings has become a true symbol of the city.

Kyoto, the cradle of Japanese culture, is also home to the oldest festival in Japan and, some say, in the world. Aoi Matsuri dates from the sixth century, when floods compelled the citizens to petition for relief the goddess of water (Tamayorihimeno Mikoto) and her son, the god of thunder (Kamo Wakeikazuchino Kami). Almost every year for the past fourteen centuries, a spring procession has been led from the Kyoto Imperial Palace to Shimogamo Shrine and Kamigamo Shrine, where they are respectively enshrined. Prayers are offered, as well, for an abundant rice harvest, so dependent on fickle nature. Leaves of *aoi* (wild ginger), a legendary deterrent to thunder, adorn eaves along the procession route, as well as the costumes of the participants. An imperial messenger on horseback leads the way, followed by an ox-drawn, lacquered cart heavily hung with wisteria. Although the festival's origins are much earlier, the accompanying retinue wear the deep-sleeved brocade robes typical of the late Heian era the tenth and eleventh centuries when Japanese cultural refinement was at its apogee.

The small mountain city of Nikkō in Tochigi Prefecture presents a comparable spectacle of its own, but with a martial theme. The resplendent Tōshōgū Shrine is the final resting place of the Edo era shogun and unifier of Japan, Tokugawa Ieyasu. In 1617 his remains were brought to Nikkō in a grand procession befitting his rank. There he was enshrined, deified, and worshiped as a *kami*, as is customary in Japan for exceedingly great personages. Every year in the months of May and October when spring and autumn are in their glory, this Thousand Man Procession (Sennin Gyōretsu) is reenacted.

Offerings are placed on the altar, sacred Shinto dances are performed, and a spirited and skillful exhibition of ancient-style equestrian archery (*yabusame*) is given, all seeking to please and entertain the deities. The procession begins with parish dignitaries on horseback leading companies of samurai soldiers and guardsmen, fitted out in authentic military manner of that bygone time: armored, helmeted, and bearing spears, halberds, bows and arrows, or matchlock guns. There are falconers and flag-bearers, masked lions, monkeys and fairies, with Shinto priests, sacred shrine maidens, pages, and traditional musicians adding to the numbers. Last of all come three *mikoshi*, the portable shrines which house the deities, including the sacred spirit of Ieyasu, for the duration of the festival. Crowded up and down the avenue are many thousands of spectators who, for a short time, feel their nation's illustrious history come to life.

Japanese festivals have always changed with the times. While those no longer relevant adapted or disappeared, new ones developed to meet certain spiritual and community needs. In 1989 Tokyo established an elaborate procession of its own, Jidai Matsuri (Festival of the Ages), patterning it after a great event of the same name in Kyoto. In the name of Tokyo's cultural renaissance, the parade reviews history from the days when the city was called Edo. Here in this great metropolis, where three out of four residents have their roots elsewhere, an event of this nature endeavors to engender a greater sense of community. Although not religiously inspired, like several other city festivals of recent genesis around Japan, religion is not forgotten here, either. The procession is tied to other events at Sensōji, Tokyo's oldest Buddhist temple, thereby bringing many worshipers among the spectators to temple precincts. In proper *matsuri* tradition, mercantile interests are also satisfied, for on that day the shops and stalls on temple grounds and in the neighborhood do exceedingly fine business.

At any festival, both place and intermediaries must first undergo ritual purification before seeking the favor of the divine world. The deity is invited to descend to the festival site, where glorious praises are offered in prayer (*norito*). Generous offerings must be made in the course of the festival's events—from the best of food and drink placed on shrine altars to sacred music, dance, drama, and other entertainments performed within the sacred boundaries of the shrine. The parading of the *mikoshi*, the elaborate and weighty portable shrine and momentary home of the honored deity, is frequently the festival highlight. With the *mikoshi* borne through the neighborhood on the striving shoulders of a multitude of somewhat intoxicated celebrants, this is no solemn procession. The unrestrained, nearly ecstatic, drum-beating, chanting, cheering, and jostling are thought to be pleasing to the gods. Sharing the burden of this tremendous weight is considered a privilege by the bearers, and the feat is cathartic, effecting physical and spiritual renewal of both bearers and their enthusiastic observers.

Official festival participants meet the gods wearing the proper garments, showing the careful attention to form demonstrated in all aspects of Japanese life. Only the finest materials and workmanship are evident, with garments most often of pure silk in the richest weave and made in traditional ceremonial style. No expense is spared in the veneration of the deities, particularly in these quite affluent times.

Matsuri are the happiest and most optimistic of occasions, when personal cares are momentarily forgotten. Customarily extremely reserved, the Japanese people then appear at their sociable best, emboldened by joy, the strength of numbers, and perhaps by some sanctified *sake*, too. Festival visitors, including foreigners, are unquestionably welcome, and their sincere interest in the proceedings often generates a quiet pride among the celebrants. These are not secret rites for believers or initiates only, but celebrations for all who care to partake.

An indivisible part of Japanese life, festivals evolve with the times, embodying the concerns of the people. Constant throughout the thousands of festivals is the ardent appeal for good luck, health, and prosperity. In the past when life was difficult for most, well-being seemed wholly at the mercy of the *kami*, yet even today, the protection and sense of security they offer maintain their appeal.

Matsuri are a visually compelling admixture of ritual, symbol, costume, and color. Anchoring the present to the past and the secular to the religious, they play a notable part in the spiritual, cultural and social life of the nation.

The ceremonial *kanmuri* headdress is the mark of a Shinto priest. Its striking design derives from the *kanmuri* all noblemen were required to wear as part of court dress in ancient times.
Saru-Saï, Kasuga Taisha, Nara

Chigo-no-Mai, an offertory dance, has been performed at the foot of Mount Fuji to appease the deity of the volcano for over a millenium. This young girl is one of a group chosen and purified at the shrine for the honor. *Chigo-no-Mai, Magomi-Sai, Kawaguchi Sengen Jinja, Yamanashi*

Believers hold the treasured medieval *gyōdō* masks they will wear in the Procession of Bodhisattvas. The procession recalls the twenty-five Buddhist saints who descended to earth in the eighth century to welcome the soul of Chūjō Hime, a local saint, which was bound for Paradise. *Neri Kuyō, Taimadera, Taima, Nara*

A Buddhist prayer is weighted by a bronze *vajra*, a ritual sceptre symbolizing absolute power. Its name comes from Sanskrit, reflecting the Indian origins of Buddhism. *Hi Watari, Takaosan, Tokyo*

In flower-bedecked hats and sheer *chihaya*, women take part in an offertory procession for the gods, one of numerous celebratory and ritual events held during the month-long festival. *Shinsen Gyōretsu, Gion Matsuri, Kyoto*

A costumed child musician plays the bamboo *bōzasara* in accompaniment to a dragon dance, performed in a bid to stop the long rains of early summer. *Mizudome-no-Mai, Gonshōji, Tokyo*

A little girl clutches her bag of *chitose ame* (thousand-year candy) at the Seven-Five-Three child-blessing festival. *Shichi-Go-San, Shinshōji, Narita, Chiba*

Offered prayer cloths surround the bell cord which is pulled to call the attention of the gods at a Shinto shrine. *Kainan Jinja, Misaki, Kanagawa*

Straw folk sandals (*waraji*) of days gone by and split-toed socks (*tabi*) are the essential footwear for many a festival.

Priests stand with dignity, ceremonial maces in hand, at a Shinto rite of purification.
Sannō Matsuri, Hie Jinja, Tokyo

A banner depicting the courageous samurai of old decorates the home of a boy child for Boys' Day. Although renamed Children's Day, the festival remains strictly for boys only. *Kodomo-no-Hi, Chichibu, Saitama*

In honor of the local shrine god, hundreds of flaming torches are carried through the streets of Kurama each autumn to ecstatic chants of "Sai-rei, sai-ryō!"
Kurama Hi Matsuri, Kurama, Kyoto

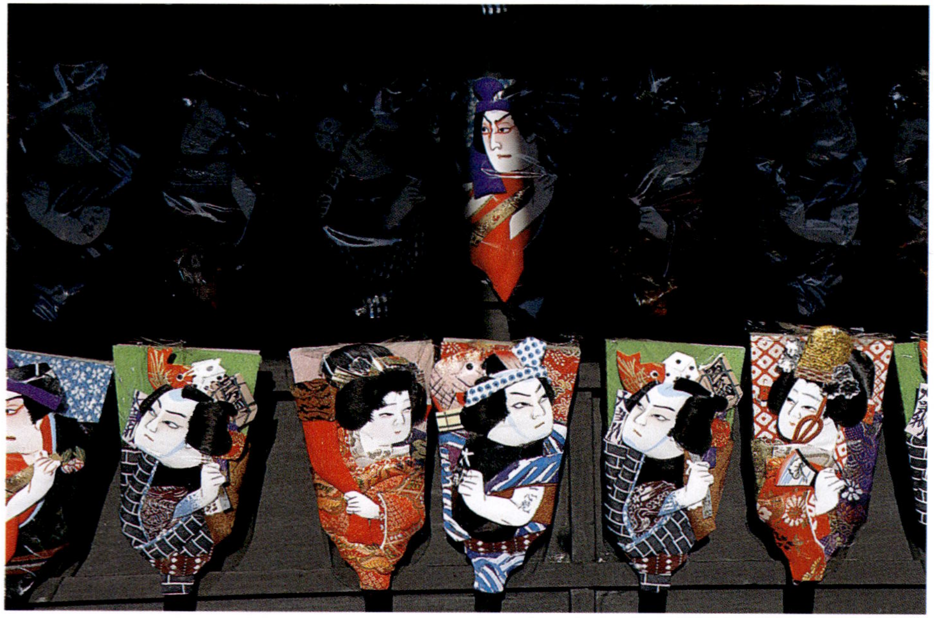

Hagoita, decorative battledores depicting kabuki characters, are on display at a New Year temple fair. Now most often purchased as holiday decorations, they were once popularly used to play the elegant badmintonlike game of *hanetsuki* on New Year's Day. *Hagoita Ichi, Asakusa, Tokyo*

A child helper to an *oiran* (a high-class courtesan), this *kamuro* is responsible for bearing the paraphernalia of her mistress, such as her cushion, pipe, and musical instruments. *Jidai Matsuri, Tokyo*

Shrine priests light lantern candles to comfort the soul of a female court attendant of ancient times who drowned herself in a pond out of unrequited love for the emperor. *Uneme Matsuri, Sarusawa Pond, Nara*

The *tomoe* and *mokkō* crests, symbols of the shrine, decorate a festival umbrella. Existing in a multitude of subtle variations, these crests were used by aristocratic families to decorate garments and belongings, even armor. They were also bestowed upon temples and shrines as a sign of patronage. *Gion Matsuri, Yasaka Jinja, Kyoto*

All of Japan, including this poodle, takes on a festive spirit during cherry blossom time, when the arrival of spring and the beauty of nature are celebrated in shrine or temple gardens and parks. *Chidorigafuchi, Tokyo*

At one of Tokyo's most famous summer festivals, a huge *mikoshi* weighing four tons—reputedly the heaviest in the city—is maneuvered through the neighborhood streets. *Torigoe Matsuri, Tokyo*

Dressed in their festive kimono, young women tie their New Year fortune papers (*o-mikuji*) to a bush in shrine precincts, hoping that the *kami* will fulfill auspicious predictions and annul less favorable ones. *Heian Jinja, Kyoto*

Honoring the temple's ancient legend in which a golden dragon appeared to protect the statue of the goddess of mercy found in the river by fishermen, the Golden Dragon Dance is performed several times each year. Dancers manipulate the fifteen-meter-long creature causing it to weave and undulate, its golden scales flashing in the sun, as it seeks to follow a golden lotus ball, the symbol of the goddess. *Kinryū-no-Mai, Sensōji, Tokyo*

Wearing vermilion ceremonial robes, priest-dancers called *mai-bito* greet the procession at the shrine's *torii* gate. This annual festival reenacts a sixth-century imperial plea to the gods to end heavy rains and flooding. *Aoi Matsuri, Shimogamo Jinja, Kyoto*

Dating from 1962, this festival was established both to attract tourism and to bond urban and rural inhabitants of the prefecture in a celebration of their common ancestry. The hemp costumes represent an ancient tumulus culture, when burial mounds of the elite were decorated with symbolic clay guardian figures called *haniwa*. *Haniwa Matsuri, Shibayama, Chiba*

An *umaosa chigo* (sacred child on horseback) rides in this offertory procession to Yasaka Shrine. His beautiful ceremonial garments are, themselves, offerings to the deities. *Hanagasa Junkō, Gion Matsuri, Kyoto*

At the pond's edge, a child performs an offertory dance representing butterflies at play. *Yawata Hachimangū, Kyoto*

Seated in formal *seiza* position, a participant awaits blessing at an equestrian archery event. *Tsurugaoka Hachimangū, Kamakura, Kanagawa*

This exotic headdress is worn by a member of a *dengaku* troupe at the Festival of the Ages. Traditionally connected to agriculture, such troupes still perform their propitious field dances at many rural festivals. *Jidai Matsuri, Tokyo*

Coming-of-Age Day is celebrated nationwide on January 15 by those who have turned twenty during the past year. At this Buddhist temple, young Kyoto women participate in *tōshiya* (ceremonial archery) to mark the event. *Seijin-no-Hi, Sanjūsangendō, Kyoto*

Horses are honored with their own festival in this agricultural and horse-breeding region. One hundred richly caparisoned horses are ridden through fields and villages in a fifteen-kilometer procession, and thanks are given for the animals' hard labors, together with prayers for their health and well-being. With each step, the many bells make the *chagu-chagu* sound from which the event takes its name. *Chagu-Chagu Umakko, Sōzen Jinja, Morioka, Iwate*

Child attendants to the *saiō dai* (princess-priestess) bear ceremonial folding cypresswood fans called *hi ōgi*. Adding to the decorative beauty of their costumes, the fans also serve as objects of dignity before the gods. *Aoi Matsuri, Kyoto*

A pageboy wears a cluster of *katsura* leaves with a token leaf or two of *aoi*. Similar to each other in shape, the abundant *katsura* and the dwindling *aoi* are nowadays both used as symbols of this ancient festival. *Aoi Matsuri, Kyoto*

As in Kyoto's renowned festival of the same name, celebrants and floats parade through the streets in a plea to the gods for summer health, but also with a more temporal wish for fun and camaraderie. *Gion Matsuri, Narita, Chiba*

A Festival of the Ages processionist is veiled in the *mushi-no-tareginu* which in earlier times protected noblewomen from insects and undesired observation while traveling. *Jidai Matsuri, Tokyo*

Shrine bells are rung by worshipers to announce their presence to the gods and to call attention to their prayers. *Kumano Jinja, Tokyo*

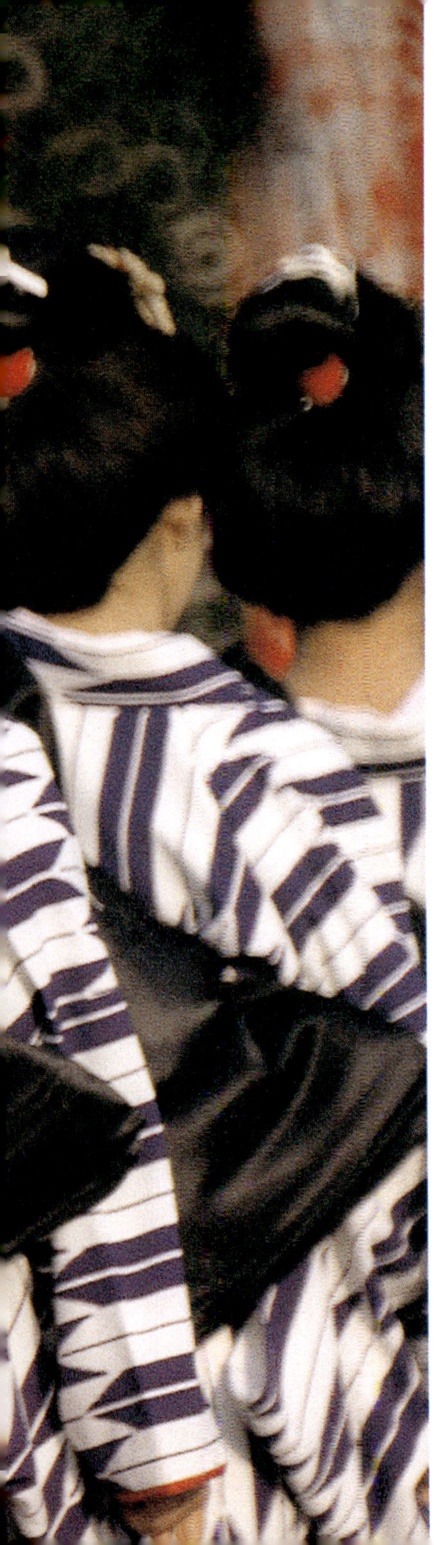

Women representing *jochū* (servants to the shogun) and attired in matching arrow feather-patterned kimono pass in procession at the Festival of the Ages. *Jidai Matsuri, Tokyo*

Depicting famous warriors and kabuki characters, these illuminated floats recall an ancient battle in which similar structures were used to trick the enemy in the manner of the Trojan horse. Providing fun before the rice harvesting begins, the festival also incorporates the *nemuri nagashi* (floating away sleep) ritual, in which floats were once set adrift at sea but are nowadays just taken for a cruise. *Nebuta Matsuri, Aomori*

Paper lanterns are hung at a family grave to light the way for spirits of ancestors and departed loved ones returning for a brief worldly visit during the Festival of the Dead.
O-Bon, Shisui, Chiba

Wearing a pocketless *yukata* robe, this festival participant uses his *hiuchi-bukuro*, once used to hold a flintstone, to carry his cigarettes and lighter. *Manto-e, Yaho Tenmangū, Kunitachi, Tokyo*

Chūjō Hime, a noblewoman who entered the temple nunnery in the eighth century, is commemorated at this festival. Miracles are attributed to her, and it is believed that on this anniversary of her death, she returns to earth to escort souls to Paradise. In a procession led by the head priest, the goddess Kannon bears the lotus throne topped by a tiny figure of Chūjō Hime. They are followed by twenty-four other believers, each representing different bodhisattvas. By their devout participation, these believers seek to save their own souls. *Neri Kuyō, Taimadera, Taima, Nara*

Tokyo tots parade at the Flower Festival, held in honor of the anniversary of Buddha's birth. It is celebrated on April 8 at many of the nation's temples with floral tributes, processions of children, and ritual bathing of an infant Buddha figurine in sweet hydrangea tea. *Hana Matsuri, Sensōji, Tokyo*

A smiling courtesan attendant takes part in Tokyo's Festival of the Ages. Dating only from 1989, this new festival celebrates the city's history. *Jidai Matsuri, Tokyo*

A team of young girls beats festival drums at a temple in commemoration of Buddha's birthday. *Hana Matsuri, Gokokuji, Tokyo*

A gracefully knotted cord and silken tassels adorn the draped entrance to a Buddhist temple. *Daishōin, Miyajima, Hiroshima*

Aoi and the look-alike *katsura* leaves embellish a brilliant robe. Four thousand branches are used in the course of this ancient festival, decorating costumes, buildings, and shrines. *Aoi Matsuri, Kyoto*

願いごと
息子が
志望校に
合格できますように
長者山
新羅神社
奉納
長者山
新羅神社

In the depths of winter, villagers hold the age-old Emburi Matsuri. Through dance, prayer plaques called *ema*, and relevant symbolism, an ardent appeal is made for the renewed fertility of the land. *Hachinohe, Aomori*

At a purification rite of fire-walking, an ascetic Buddhist mountain priest (*yamabushi*) beats the drum while others chant, creating a powerfully mystical atmosphere. *Hi Watari, Takaosan, Tokyo*

Archers are seated in ceremonial formation at a New Year's rite to dispel evil and make way for good fortune in the coming year. *Momote-shiki, Meiji Jingū, Tokyo*

O-Bon, the summer Festival of the Dead observed all across Japan, possesses a unique South Seas flavor on these islands off the coast of Kyushu. Almost unchanged for eight centuries, the rites maintain the ancient forms brought from the Chinese mainland, with drumming and the chanting of sutras to awaken and welcome the spirits of ancestors. In Tamanoura on Gotō Island, a grass-skirted procession is led through the village, while on Saganoshima, a ritual dance is performed at the shore. *O-Bon, Gotō Rettō, Nagasaki*

A shrine princess (*yaotome*) mounts her horse for a procession, part of a lavish four-day festival in honor of the deity who ended the famine of 1136. *On Matsuri, Kasuga Wakamiya Jinja, Nara*

In thanks to the gods for an abundant harvest, sanctified children perform a ritualized field dance. *Ta-Mai, Zuiki Matsuri, Kitano Tenmangū, Kyoto*

Ceremonial oiled paper umbrellas decorated with strips of sacred paper are carried by processionists. *On Matsuri, Kasuga Wakamiya Jinja, Nara*

A masked dancer performs *bugaku* in ancient imperial court style. He wears a helmet bearing a stylized image of the auspicious phoenix and dances in praise of eternal heaven and earth. *Haru Matsuri, Meiji Jingū, Tokyo*

The dancer's silk robe is embroicered with the *mokkō* crest, a popular motif on Japanese court costumes since the sixth century, when it was adopted from China. *Haru Matsuri, Meiji Jingū, Tokyo*

Koi nobori (carp streamers) fly against the spectacular backdrop of sacred Mount Fuji in celebration of Boys' Day. Despite the twentieth-century change of name to Children's Day, the festival remains boy-oriented, and the streamers express the wish that boys of the household will grow up to be as healthy and vigorous as the carps that swim upstream. *Kodomo-no-Hi, Asagiri Kōgen, Shizuoka*

As part of New Year festivities, archers perform the first archery of the year in a ceremony of blessing and symbolic deflection of evil. *Tsurugaoka Hachimangū, Kamakura, Kanagawa*

Martial paraphernalia and a ceremonial drum are set aside during a break in festivities.
Sennin Gyōretsu, Tōshōgū, Nikkō, Tochigi

White horses, long regarded as sacred messengers of the gods, were once valued offerings to Shinto shrines from wealthy parishioners. With time, wooden statues of horses came to be offered instead, eventually evolving into votive tablets bearing only the picture of a horse. These are the origin of *ema*, so-called horse picture prayer plaques, which today depict a huge diversity of images, but rarely the horse.
Suwa Taisha, Nagano

A sanctified child made up in ancient style wears plum blossoms, the symbol of the celebrating shrine, in her hair.
Zuiki Matsuri, Kitano Tenmangū, Kyoto

Immortalizing Lady Fujiwara, a thirteenth-century poet, the Festival of the Ages represents her in the style of traveling clothes she might have worn on her trip to Kamakura, when she wrote the travel diary for which she is known. *Jidai Matsuri, Kyoto*

Representing *komusō* (Zen Buddhist mendicant monks of the past), these processionists wear the concealing basketlike head coverings required of the monks when outside temple walls. They play the *shakuhachi* (bamboo flutes) which earned the monks their alms. *Jidai Matsuri, Tokyo*

Branches of artificial wisteria cast their shadows upon the bamboo shades of the *gosho-guruma* (imperial cart). *Aoi Matsuri, Kyoto*

Helping hands working together support the festival *mikoshi* (sacred shrine palanquin) which can weigh as much as several tons. *Kanamara Matsuri, Kawasaki, Kanagawa*

A festival musician wears a *yukata* robe bearing images of the rain dragon and its scales at a festival held to stop the heavy rains of early summer. *Mizudome-no-Mai, Gonshōji, Tokyo*

A young celebrant has found a quiet spot to rest, away from the festival uproar. *Gion Matsuri, Narita, Chiba*

At a rural Shinto festival, a *kagura* dance performer wears the Okame mask symbolizing happiness and prosperity.
Shishi-Mai, Chichibu, Saitama

Huge straw boats bedecked with written prayers to Buddha are set adrift in celebration of O-Bon, the summer Festival of the Dead. The coiled prow ornament represents an elephant's trunk, a Buddhist symbol. *Shaarabune, Nishinoshima, Shimane*

A *geisha*, one of a group performing traditional flute, *shamisen* and *taiko* music, takes part in the Golden Dragon Dance. *Kinryū-no-Mai, Sensōji, Tokyo*

On Coming-of-Age Day, young Tokyo women pose for proud parents' cameras by the lantern at Meiji Shrine. *Seijin-no-Hi, Meiji Jingū, Tokyo*

Body tattooing has been elevated to an art in Japan. Nowadays, it is the hallmark of *yakuza* gang members, as these *mikoshi* bearers are likely to be. More tolerated than their Western counterparts, they sometimes bare their tattoos at summer festivals.

Wearing ceremonial vestments and cloglike *asagutsu*, priests of Meiji Shrine walk in festival procession. *Meiji Jingū, Tokyo*

Bugaku dancers perform for the *kami* of the shrine. This ancient Japanese imperial court style of dance has roots that go even further back to China. *Aki Matsuri, Meiji Jingū, Tokyo*

Mifune Matsuri reenacts an afternoon of Heian court amusement on the Ōi River. Twenty boats, some with magnificent figureheads depicting mythical creatures, carry celebrants slowly down the river. Dressed in period costume, they engage in a variety of elegant pastimes and entertainment. A special sacred boat carries child dancers who, dressed as *karyōbin* (birds of legend), perform to the sacred tunes of court music.
Mifune Matsuri, Kyoto

The back of a celebrant's *kamishimo* robe is adorned with plum crests, as well as a branch of artificial red plum blossoms.
Yamaboko Junkō, Gion Matsuri, Kyoto

A traditional oiled paper umbrella, one of a Gion processionist's accessories, is traced with the delicate pattern of wisteria.
Hanagasa Junkō, Gion Matsuri, Kyoto

At the close of the month-long Gion Matsuri, the legendary "umbrella heron" (*kasa-sagi*) is commemorated in a dance for once protecting a Buddhist priest from the rain by spreading its wings overhead. *Sagi-Mai, Gion Matsuri, Yasaka Jinja, Kyoto*

This procession of *oiran* (high-class courtesans) was one of real-life courtesans in the Edo era. Their extravagantly high and heavy footwear (*mitsuba geta*) cause the stylized, dragging gait which emphasizes their role as objects of entertainment and pleasure. Their hairstyles are similarly emblematic.
Oiran Dōchū, Tokyo

The courtesan's wig is dressed in the traditional *tate hyōgo* style and accented with ornamental tortoiseshell combs and picks, with titillating strands of hair left hanging loose. *Oiran Dōchū, Tokyo*

An altar of ritual offerings is flanked by fan-decorated standards (*ōgi mikoshi*), inviting the god to the site of the great Nachi Fire Festival. *Nachi Hi Matsuri, Kumano Nachi Taisha, Nachi Katsuura, Wakayama*

To the clacking sound of the percussive wooden *binzasara*, dancers perform *dengaku*, an agricultural field dance, to welcome the god back to the shrine for Gion Matsuri. It is believed that the spirit of the god will descend and momentarily dwell in the sacred zig-zag papers hanging from the dancers' hats. *Gion Matsuri, Yasaka Jinja, Kyoto*

Ryūju Bosatsu, the so-called Dragon Tree Bodhisattva, walks in an attitude of prayer. This commemoration of Chūjō Hime, an eighth-century noblewoman who entered the temple nunnery, has been held every year since 1005. *Neri Kuyō, Taimadera, Taima, Nara*

Ritually purified "princesses" perform a sacred dance of harvest thanksgiving for the deities.
Zuiki Matsuri, Kitano Tenmangū, Kyoto

Buddha's birthday is marked in this out-of-the-way village with an enchanting scattering of petals by local children, recalling the blossoms which reputedly rained from the heavens when Buddha preached. This local version of the nationwide festival serves as a rite of passage for pre-teen boys.
Hana Matsuri, Tsukagoshi, Chichibu, Saitama

The festival procession returns to the shrine following the spring rice-planting ceremony in the shrine's sacred rice paddy. *O-Taue-Sai, Katori Jingū, Chiba*

The stylized beauty of a Kyoto *maiko* is captured in detail at a Shinto dedicatory dance performance. *Gion Matsuri, Kyoto*

Japan's oldest festival is a reenactment of a sixth-century imperial procession, but its lavish costumes exemplify the glorious culture of Heian-era aristocracy (874–1185).
Aoi Matsuri, Kyoto

Mibu kyōgen, a drama form officially designated as an Important Intangible Cultural Asset, consists of pantomimical performances relating the teachings of Buddha. In this festival dramatization of the Earth Spider parable *Tsuchi-Gumo*, victory of good over evil is memorably portrayed. *Mibudera, Kyoto*

The face of a kabuki villain, identifiable by the blue lines of viciousness on his face, decorates a New Year battledore for sale at a festive year-end fair. *Hagoita Ichi, Asakusa, Tokyo*

Commemorating a local Buddhist legend, a fox-bride and fox-groom are wed in the presence of numerous fox-attendants. Yet in accordance with Shinto tradition, the wedding vows are sealed with ritual sips of *sake* from red lacquered cups. This syncretic celebration honors long and faithful marriages, while also marking the successful autumn harvest. *Kitsune-no-Yomeiri, Hōjōji, Kudamatsu, Yamaguchi*

A feudal equestrian archer's gear includes the hide of a deer, which not only offers physical protection, but is also symbolic of speed and grace. The auspicious golden dragonfly at his wrist represents victory, an association stemming from one of the insect's alternate names. *Yabusame, Tsurugaoka Hachimangū, Kamakura, Kanagawa*

Wearing the lacquered wooden *asagutsu* of his office, a priest strides across shrine grounds. *Aoi Matsuri, Kamigamo Jinja, Kyoto*

A family enjoys an evening in their snow hut (*kamakura*) beneath the castle on the hill. During the festival, offerings are placed within the hut in honor of the deity of water, while kids enjoy grilling and eating *mochi* rice cakes, drinking sweet *ama-zake,* and playing card games known as *karuta.*
Kamakura Matsuri, Yokote, Akita

Hundreds of blazing torches light up the night at this fire festival. Honoring the local shrine god, the event originated as a tenth-century initiation rite. *Kurama Hi Matsuri, Yuki Jinja, Kurama, Kyoto*

This festival *mikoshi* is completely decorated with local agricultural products in thanksgiving for a bountiful harvest. *Zuiki Matsuri, Tenmangū, Kyoto*

Straw-hatted Edo-era footmen bear the traveling supply baskets of their masters at the Festival of the Ages. *Jidai Matsuri, Kyoto*

The beautiful and brave Tomoe Gozen, legendary twelfth-century warrior and concubine to General Minamcto, is portrayed on horseback. *Jidai Matsuri, Kyoto*

A processionist represents the beloved bodhisattva Jizō-san, protector of children and travelers. *Neri Kuyō, Taimadera, Taima, Nara*

A three-year-old girl, accompanied by her family and dog, visits Hie Shrine to receive Shinto blessings during the Seven-Five-Three Festival. *Shichi-Go-San, Hie Jinja, Tokyo*

The founder of the Buddhist Agon sect wields his ritual sceptre (*vajra*) to dispel evil influences at the Star Festival. *Hoshi Matsuri, Yamashina, Kyoto*

Dressed as armored samurai, participants march in commemoration of the 350-kilometer procession bearing the ashes of Tokugawa Ieyasu to Tōshō Shrine. *Sennin Gyōretsu, Tōshōgū, Nikkō, Tochigi*

A Kyoto beauty represents a princess-priestess of the ancient festival. She wears the imperial headdress symbolic of the sun, the same privilege accorded to her predecessors centuries before.
Aoi Matsuri, Kyoto

Recreating a Heian-era amusement, participants in noble garb of the day sit beside a stream writing *tanka* poems. Once a poem is completed, the writer has earned a sip from one of the *sake* cups floating down the stream. *Kyokusui-no-en, Jōnangū, Kyoto*

A disciple of Izumono Okuni, the sixteenth-century shrine maiden who performed sacred dances and is credited with creating kabuki, is among the innumerable historical characters portrayed at the Festival of the Ages. *Jidai Matsuri, Kyoto*

The imperial procession is symbolically protected by mounted archers carrying quivers on their backs. *Aoi Matsuri, Kyoto*

Everyone takes off their shoes to sit on tarpaulins under the cherry trees for O-Hanami, one of the most joyous and spontaneous events of the festival calendar. These *zōri* sandals were set here by one of a group of elderly women who came to enjoy a picnic and some traditional dance under the blossoms. *O-Hanami, Sumida Kōen, Tokyo*

Processioning court attendants are attired in multi-layered silk robes. The outer ones are made of *nishiki* (Japanese brocade) and are often richly woven with threads of gold and silver. *Aoi Matsuri, Kyoto*

Representatives from five of Kyoto's parishes await the imperial messenger bearing precious gifts for the *kami*. *Aoi Matsuri, Shimogamo Jinja, Kyoto*

First organized by local fishermen over 150 years ago, the Naked Festival continues to implore the deities to provide bountiful catches. Sacred *mikoshi*, the temporary dwellings of the gods, are borne into the waves, delighting the gods, participants, and the hundreds of photographers who converge there every year. *Hadaka Matsuri, Ōhara, Chiba*

An *oiran*, a high-class courtesan of the Edo era, walks regally in festival procession beneath the *janome*, a bamboo and paper umbrella held for her by an attendant. *Oiran Dōchū, Tokyo*

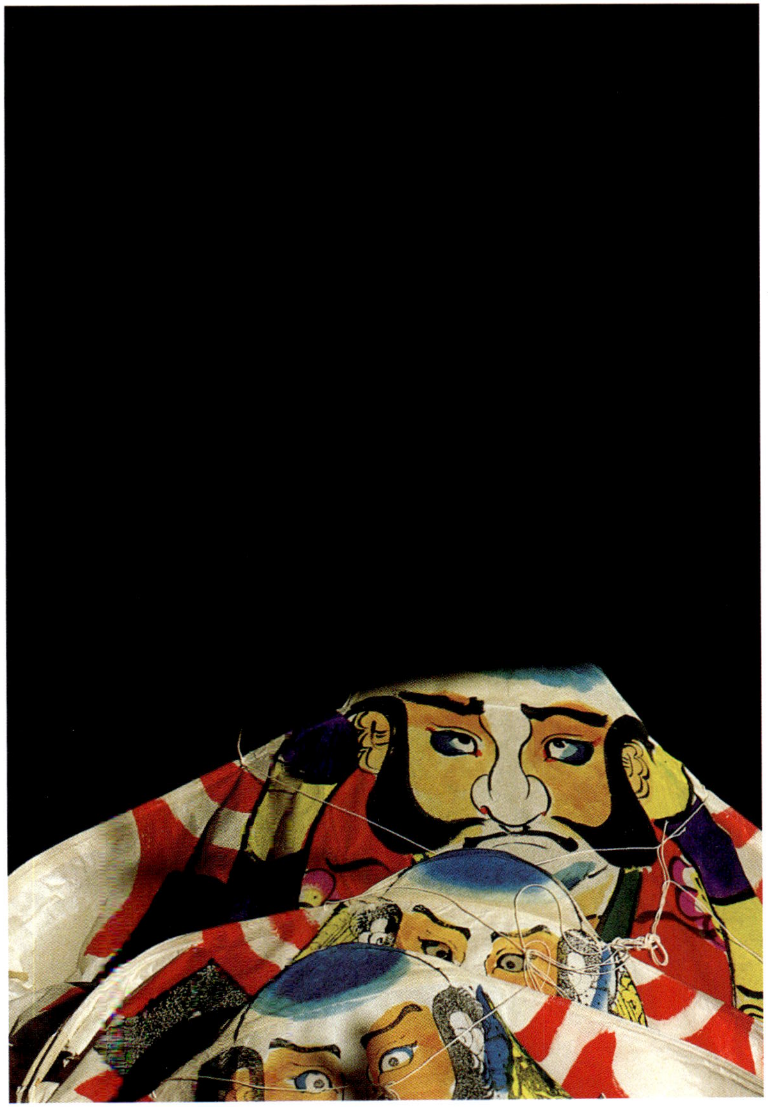

Glowering faces of *yakko* (samurai attendants) stare out from paper kites, sold as talismans against fire. *Tako Ichi, Ōji Inari Jinja, Tokyo*

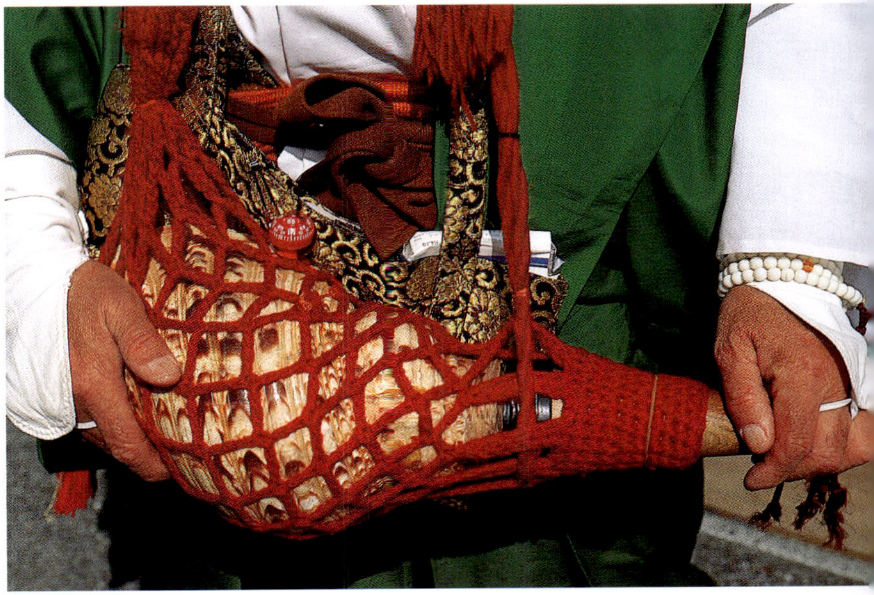

A mountain priest bears a great conch shell, regarded as a sacred object since ancient times because its clockwise spiral connects it with the course of the sun. Used as a simple wind instrument, its portentous sound is said to represent the voice of Buddha. *Hi Watari, Takaosan, Tokyo*

A festival organizer wears the customary *happi* coat. The Chinese characters on the back identify him as a member of the number four *mikoshi* group. *Kanamara Matsuri, Kawasaki, Kanagawa*

Sacred offerings of *sake*, water, salt, and seaweed are placed on the festival *mikoshi* to honor the deity within. *Sannō Matsuri, Hie Jinja, Tokyo*

The Mud Festival is celebrated in homage to fertility and the "five grains." Local young men who plan to marry during the next year douse the sacred *mikoshi* in a muddy stream, while youths good-naturedly throw mud at them and shout double entendres. *Doronko Matsuri, Noda, Chiba*

Dressed in ceremonial regalia, the head priest of the temple conducts a requiem mass for the repose of the souls of used and broken needles. *Hari Kuyō, Shōjuin, Tokyo*

In a festival of midsummer purification, male parishioners carry the sacred *mikoshi* around the tiny island. Sprayed with water by enthusiastic celebrants along the way, the palanquin is ultimately taken for a ritual dip into the bay. *Natsu Matsuri, Enoshima, Kanagawa*

A Kyoto *maiko* (apprentice *geisha*) dances for the gods among a host of dedicatory performances, both traditional and modern, performed in honor of Heian Shrine's centenary. *Heian Jingū, Kyoto*

A dancer at a Meiji Shrine festival performs a *bugaku* dance of Chinese origin, representing cranes fishing for carp in waters of plenitude. *Haru Matsuri, Meiji Jingū, Tokyo*

The striking crested *horo*, the protective mantle once worn by samurai over bamboo basketlike armor, is part of a processionist's garb. *Gion Matsuri, Kyoto*

Festival lanterns hang from the eaves of a splendid float. *Yayoi Matsuri, Nikkō, Tochigi*

A mounted Heian-era official wears brocade-cuffed, lacquered leather boots called *kanokutsu*, designed after the onetime footgear of Mongolian riders. *Aoi Matsuri, Kyoto*

An orange silk umbrella imprinted with the name Ayagasa Boko, one of more than thirty magnificent floats in the procession, is made luminous by the sun above.
Gion Matsuri, *Kyoto*

Wearing traditional festive finery, a child visits a Shinto shrine to receive blessings for health and happiness during the Seven-Five-Three Festival. *Shichi-Go-San, Hie Jinja, Tokyo*

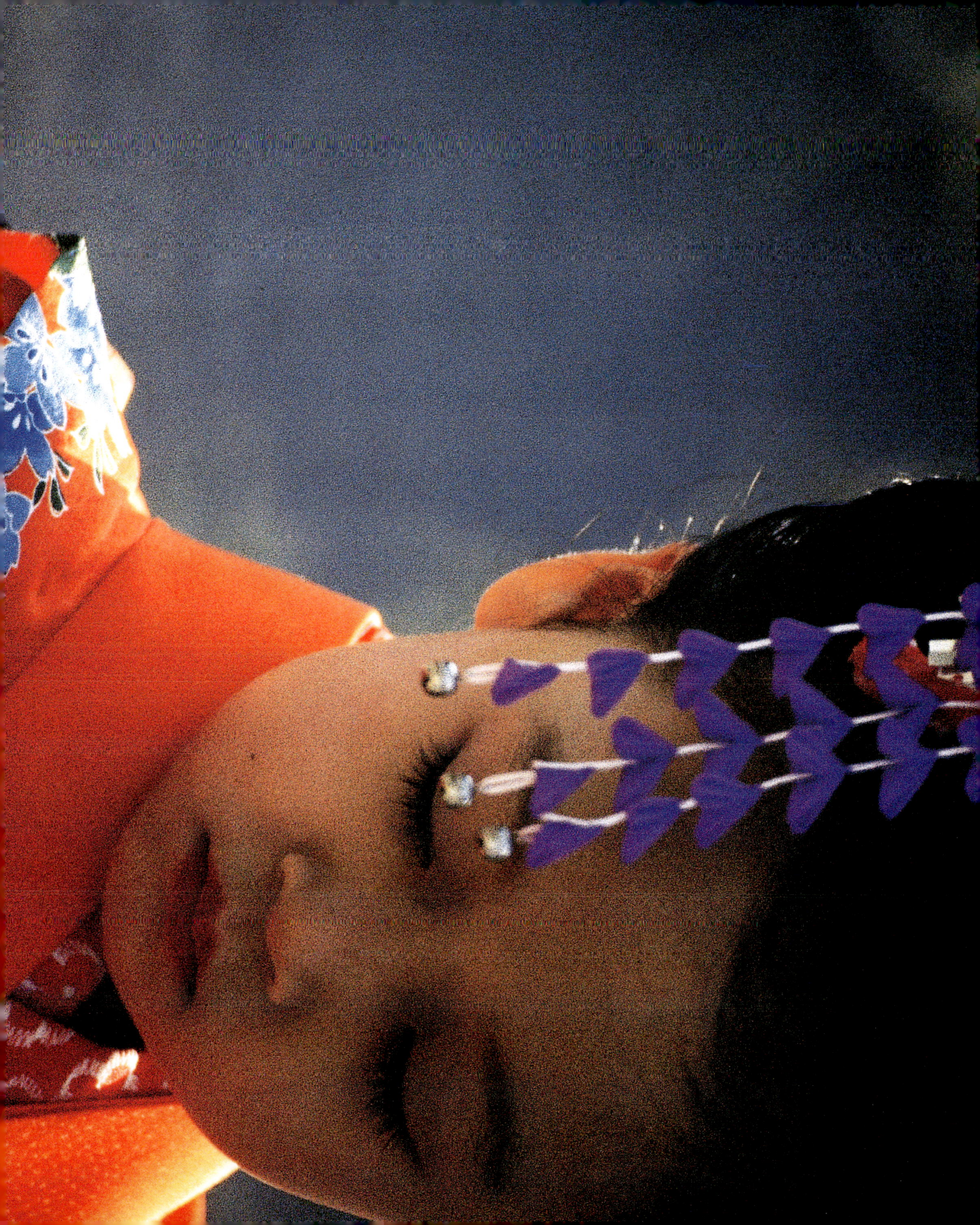

Mounted female guards in Heian-era garments ride in attendance to the *saiō dai*, a princess-priestess of the age-old festival. *Aoi Matsuri, Kyoto*

A participant in the role of a feudal-era court lady is shielded from the gaze of lesser mortals and the annoyance of insects by her *mushi-no-tareginu*, aristocratic travel attire of the day. *Sannō Matsuri, Hie Jinja, Tokyo*

The presentation of sacred offerings is an integral element of every *matsuri*. These artfully arranged fruits of land, sea, and mountain are meant to please the deity of the shrine. *Aoi Matsuri, Shimogamo Jinja, Kyoto*

At lunar new year, small dog figurines and other offerings are presented together with prayers for good luck at snow huts serving as temporary shrines. This Little Dog Festival derives from a time in the past when, plagued with robberies, the local folk sculpted small, talismanic watchdogs from rice paste. *Inukko Matsuri, Yuzawa, Akita*

In this Kyushu midsummer festival, ritually purified women carry food into the rice field to feed the gods, thus ensuring the crop's continuing healthy growth. *Onda-Sai, Kumamoto*

At a rural lion dance celebration, a musician's face is screened by a bamboo and cloth headdress bearing the shrine's name.
Shishi-Mai, Muku Jinja, Chichibu, Saitama

Wearing splendid woven leather armor lacquered in an auspicious martial pattern, the fourteenth-century Lord Kusunoki is represented triumphally entering Kyoto. *Jidai Matsuri, Kyoto*

A Kyoto *maiko* ties her *ema* (prayer plaque) for the attention of the gods at the Comb Festival, held to comfort the souls of old and broken combs. *Kushi Matsuri, Kompira Jinja, Kyoto*

No longer the *chigo* (sacred child), the little boy sits on the bus, waiting to go home. *Hana Matsuri, Gokokuji, Tokyo*

A young *uneme* rides on her father's shoulders. Believed able to communicate with the deities, she carries young rice plants in appeal for a rich harvest. *Onda-Sai, Matsuo Taisha, Kyoto*

Dressed in underrobes, the *saiō dai* (princess-priestess) displays her lengthy cascade of hair while waiting to don the *jūni hitoe*, twelve layers of robes weighing over thirty pounds. *Aoi Matsuri, Kyoto*

Miko (shrine maidens) enact the rice-planting process at this Shinto spring festival. By means of this form of imitative magic, success is sought for the soon-to-be-planted rice crop. *Haru Matsuri, Kasuga Taisha, Nara*

A lantern is silhouetted against a vivid silk festival drape in the late afternoon sun.
Toyokawa Inari Jinja, Tokyo

Yoshino Tayū, a high-ranked courtesan of the seventeenth century renowned for her great beauty and wit, is immortalized at the Festival of the Ages. *Jidai Matsuri, Kyoto*

Equestrian archery (*yabusame*) is said to date back to the sixth century, when it was practiced as a rite of divination. Later developed as a samurai skill, *yabusame* performances may nowadays be dedicated to the god of war and are held to dispel evil. *Yabusame, Tsurugaoka Hachimangū, Kamakura, Kanagawa*

Honoring a twelfth-century act of filial piety when two samurai warriors, the Soga brothers, avenged their father's assassination, this festival includes the warriors and their mother among the characters represented. Paper umbrellas are ritually burned and memorialized, recalling the umbrella-torches used in the attack. *Soga-no-Kasayaki Matsuri, Jōzenji, Odawara, Kanagawa*

An *umaosa chigo* (sacred child on horseback) carries a basket of irises on his back. Known as flowers of purification, they were once believed to ward off plague and demons. *Hanagasa Junkō, Gion Matsuri, Kyoto*

A Buddhist priest wears ceremonial *soai* clogs which are covered in metallic brocade.
Nijūgo Bosatsu O-Neri Kuyō, Dainembutsuji, Osaka

Dolls are offered on Girls' Day, together with prayers to the enshrined deity, guardian of women. *Hina Matsuri, Awashima Jinja, Wakayama*

A pageboy, one of twelve in attendance at the Thousand Man Procession, wears a robe of the finest silk brocade. *Sennin Gyōretsu, Nikkō, Tochigi*

A *shakujō* (sistrum), a ritual object symbolizing holiness, wisdom, and the power of exorcism, is held by an ascetic mountain priest. *Hi Matsuri, Chichibu, Saitama*

The splendid floats of Gion Matsuri are decorated with treasured antique textiles from Kyoto and around the world. The short hangings were once believed to attract disease-bearing spirits, which could then be ritually purified with water. *Gion Matsuri, Kyoto*

The sash (*obi*) worn around the kimono once symbolized a woman's heart and is honored at this annual festival. This woman is dressed in the fashion of the eighth-century Nara era, one of many eras represented. *Obi Matsuri, Jōshōji, Kyoto*

Meiji Shrine marks the advent of spring and autumn with spectacular festivals. Ancient and elegant court music and dance (*gagaku* and *bugaku*) with roots in Korea, China, and southeast Asia are performed by official imperial court ensembles. Splendid, authentic costumes and appurtenances abound, reminding one and all of the nation's wealth of history, culture, and religion. *Haru Matsuri, Meiji Jingū, Tokyo*

Seated within her palanquin, a young woman represents the *uneme*, a court attendant of ancient times, who committed suicide out of unrequited love for the emperor. This annual festival is held to comfort her soul. *Uneme Matsuri, Sarusawa Pond, Nara*

Dating from the eighth-century Nara era, this dance is solemnly performed by Shinto priests. With ceremonial fans and branches of the sacred evergreen *sakaki*, they dance to invoke the spirit of the land. *Yamato-Mai, Saru-Sai, Kasuga Taisha, Nara*

The *chigo,* the celestial child of the spectacular Gion Matsuri, is borne from the shrine on an attendant's shoulders, beneath a protective ceremonial umbrella. *Gion Matsuri, Kyoto*

A golden phoenix, an auspicious mythological symbol, ornaments the top of many a sacred festival *mikoshi* (palanquin of the god).

In thanks for an abundant harvest, a priest performs a field dance to the clacking rhythm of his *binzasara. Kokiriko Matsuri, Taira, Toyama*

Once a year, the mountain god is borne by *mikoshi* to see his grandchild, deity of children, who is enshrined nearby. The shrine is one of many in the vicinity of Mount Fuji which venerate the volcano as sacred. *Magomi Matsuri, Sengen Jinja, Kawaguchiko, Yamanashi*

This rare old *mikoshi* is made in the spare style of the thirteenth and fourteenth centuries. It is marked with a miniature *torii*, the sacred gate of Shinto, and bedecked with a profusion of white paper *shide*, symbols of purity and sanctity. *Magomi Matsuri, Sengen Jinja, Kawaguchiko, Yamanashi*

Elaborate carved, painted and gilded ornamentation, symbolic of flames and auspicious clouds, decorates a ceremonial *matsuri* gong. *Aoi Matsuri, Kyoto*

At crowded market stalls, holiday shoppers buy their New Year battledores, decorated with striking faces from kabuki drama and *ukiyo-e* prints of the "floating world." *Hagoita Ichi, Asakusa, Tokyo*

Color, light and shadow create art of a Buddhist priest's ceremonial robe. *Hana Matsuri, Gokokuji, Tokyo*

Apprentice *geisha* called *maiko* perform the Sparrow Dance. Based on a famous old folk tale, the dance illustrates the virtue of repaying one's obligations. *Suzume Odori, Gion Matsuri, Kyoto*

A *maiko* expresses the graceful mood of Kyoto in a dance onomatopoetically called Kon-kon-chiki-chin Kon-chiki-chin after the sound and rhythm of Gion-bayashi, the distinctive music of the festival. *Gion Matsuri, Kyoto*

Oshiroi, the white makeup of the traditional "flower and willow world," is worn by this *tayū*, the highest class of courtesan. Peaked patterns accent the beauty and eroticism of the neck, a part of the female body much appreciated by the Japanese. *Obi Matsuri, Jōshōji, Kyoto*